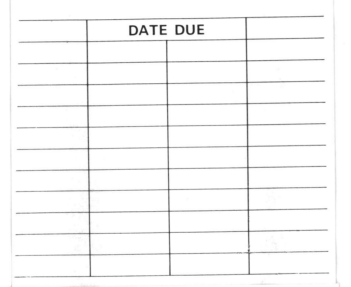

Read•A•Picture
COLORS &
NUMBERS

Library of Congress Cataloging-in-Publication Data

Marks, Burton.
    Colors & numbers / by Burton Marks; illustrated by Paul Harvey.
      p.   cm.—(Read-a-picture)
    Summary: Rebuses introduce the world of colors and provide
practice in counting.
    ISBN 0-8167-2411-3 (lib. bdg.)   ISBN 0-8167-2412-1 (pbk.)
    1. Color—Pictorial works—Juvenile literature. 2. Counting—
Pictorial works—Juvenile literature. 3. Rebuses. [1. Color.
2. Counting. 3. Rebuses.] I. Harvey, Paul, 1926-   ill.
II. Title. III. Title: Colors and numbers. IV. Series: Marks,
Burton. Read-a-picture.
QC495.5.M37 1992
535.6—dc20   91-17493

Published by Watermill Press.

Read·A·Picture
COLORS &
NUMBERS

By Burton Marks
Illustrated by Paul Harvey

Watermill Press

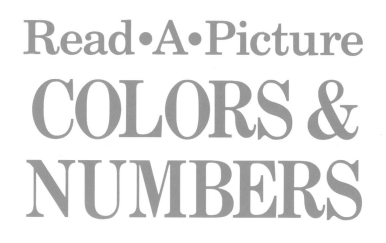

COUNTING COLORS

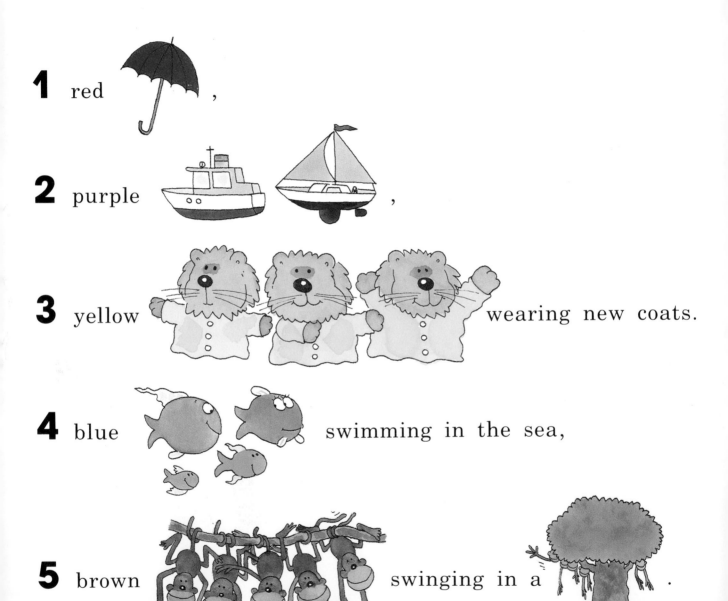

1 red   ,

2 purple   ,

3 yellow   wearing new coats.

4 blue   swimming in the sea,

5 brown   swinging in a   .

6 orange  ,

7 black  ,

8 pink
learning to dance.

9 green
riding on a train,

10 white
walking in the rain.

WHAT THINGS ARE RED?

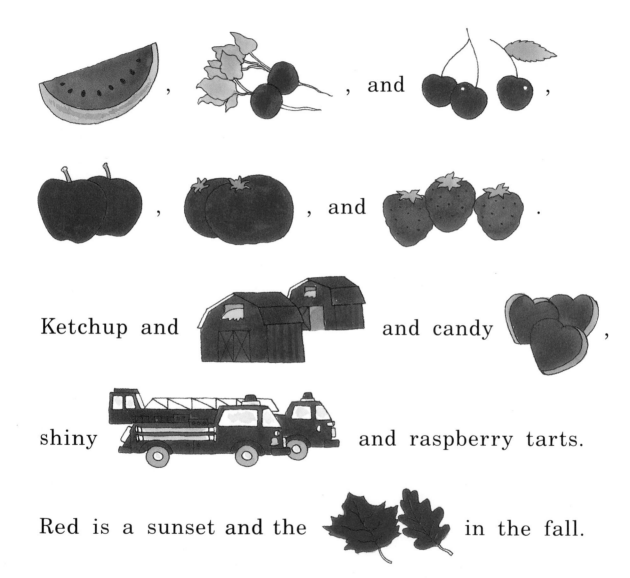

, , and , ,

, and .

Ketchup and and candy ,

shiny and raspberry tarts.

Red is a sunset and the in the fall.

Perhaps red is the prettiest color of all.

FIND-A-PICTURE

Somewhere in this picture are:

1 , **2** , **3** , **4** , and **5** . Can you find them?

WHAT THINGS ARE YELLOW?

Canaries and 🍐🍐🍐 and vanilla custard,

and 🧀🧀 and hot-dog mustard!

and 🐹🐹 and baby chicks,

and 🌽 and lemon sticks.

Yellow is candlelight, and yellow is the ☀️

that shines when I go outside to have fun.

SUE'S SHOES

One day a  whose name was Sue exclaimed, "I think I've lost a  ."

She cried out loud:

Boo hoo, boo hoo! What will I do with just one  ?

Just then a  called out, "Yoo-hoo," and straight into the room he flew—

Oh, lucky you— I found your  .

But my shoe is red.
This  is blue.
It positively
will not do.

That's true, that's true,
but let's review.
Instead of **1**
you now have **2**!

Just then a  came passing through...

My dear friend Sue,
I brought for you
a purple  —
now toodle-oo.

Oh, dear me!
How can this be?
Instead of **2**
I now have **3**.

And then a 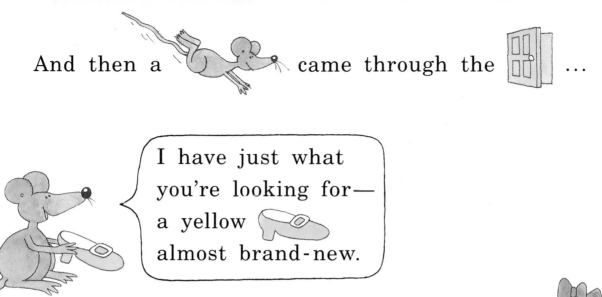 came through the ...

I have just what you're looking for— a yellow 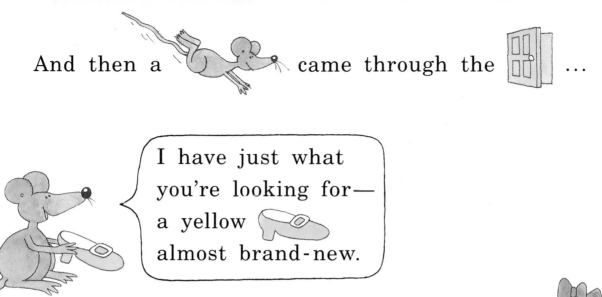 almost brand-new.

Oh, please! Don't bring me any more! Instead of **3** I now have **4**.

But then a  arrived...

Oh dear, I fear, here's number **5**.

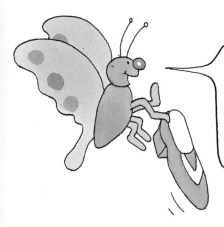

I just heard about your missing so I brought a new green one for you.

Now Sue was not ungrateful,
and she really was amused
at being the new owner
of so many pretty

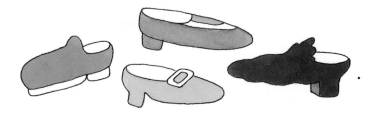

WHAT THINGS ARE BLUE?

Blue jeans, 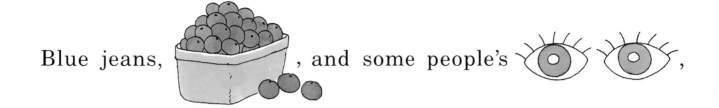, and some people's eyes,

blue and and cloudless skies,

blue 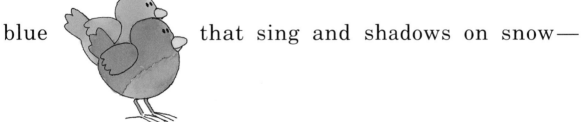 that sing and shadows on snow—

now how many more blue things do you know?

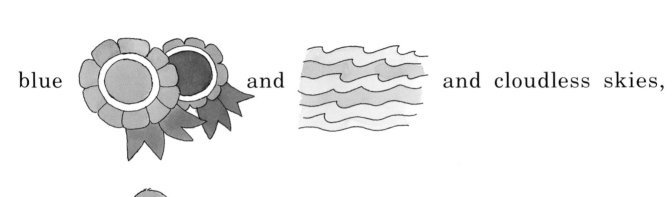

OWL'S COUNTING GAME

Here's a counting game that's fun. Let's see if you can count to one.

That's easy! I just say **1** shining  and then I'm done.

Now tell me who can count to two.

1 spool of .

2 loaves of 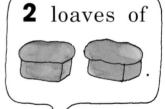.

THE RAINY DAY SURPRISE

Sometimes, on rainy days, Mother gave Tommy

a little surprise. "Will I get a surprise today?" asked

 as the 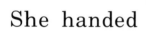 streamed down his bedroom .

"I have a colorful surprise for you," said  .

She handed 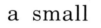 a small 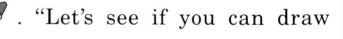 . It was a

bright new box of  . "Let's see if you can draw

things that are the same color as each in

the box," said  .

"I'll try," said ![boy] . "That sounds like fun."

First Tommy chose a ![crayon] and drew the  .

Then he took a ![crayon] and drew a ![tree] . Next

he used a ![crayon] to draw a  and a ![crayon]

to draw ![waves] . He used the ![crayon] to draw a ![pumpkin] .

Finally he used the ![crayon] to draw some .

"Now can you draw a picture using every color

in the box?" asked ![girl] . ![boy] thought for a

moment. Then he started to draw.

Can you guess what Tommy drew?
Turn the page to find the answer.

"That's a perfect picture to draw for a rainy day," said .

WHAT THINGS ARE GREEN?

and celery and pickles and   , and   and   and big leafy   ,   , olives, cabbage, and   , grasshoppers,   , and evergreens.

Green is everywhere, or so it would seem;

how many things can *you* name that are green?